Breaking the 'Optics-First' Mentality

Pulling back the curtain on personal branding and modern-day marketing.

Author: Hannah Hall

Contents

Chapter 1 1
    Breaking the 'Optics-First' Mentality 1

Chapter 2 8
    The Dark Side of Visibility – Case Studies and Consequences 8

Chapter 3 16
    Authenticity is the New Influence – Rethinking the Rules 16

Chapter 4 23
    The Publicist's Perspective – Insider Stories on the 'Game' 23

Chapter 5 30
    A Framework for Authentic Visibility–Practical Steps for Leaders 30

Chapter 38
    Building a Legacy That Lasts–Beyond the Hashtag 38

Chapter 7 47
    Leading by Example 47

Conclusion 54
    The Final Shift – From Influence to Impact 54

Book Synopsis: .... Error! Bookmark not defined.

About the Author

With over 20 years of experience in global marketing, publicity, and public relations, Hannah Hall has established herself as a trusted expert in amplifying the voices of athletes, CEOs, entrepreneurs, and organizations. As the author of *It's Donut Day, Why Aren't We Posting?* Hannah once again pulls back the curtain on personal branding and modern-day marketing, asking the critical question: *Is it possible to be seen and stay authentic?* In a world where visibility equates to power, she explores the tension between authenticity and the louder-than-life pursuit of attention, challenging the notion that shouting for attention leads to true success.

Throughout her career, Hannah has navigated the delicate line every publicist faces, balancing the creation of someone's image with maintaining her own integrity. She's seen firsthand how an *optics-first mentality* can feel safe and rewarding in the short term, yet ultimately limits those who aspire to build lasting influence. Leaders who focus solely on what looks good often miss the opportunity to cultivate true, meaningful impact.

Through her expertise in strategic storytelling, media relations, and branding, Hannah continues to guide leaders and organisations toward a more authentic, powerful presence, one that transcends surface-level optics and fosters genuine connection.

Introduction

Understanding the 'Optics-First' Mentality

In today's digital age, visibility, and recognition is everything. Whether it's through social media, media coverage, or networking, the drive to be seen often overshadows the desire to be understood. This is where the *'Optics-First'* mentality comes in. It's the idea that appearances, impressions, and surface-level success are the ultimate measures of achievement. We live in a world where looking successful is often more important than being successful, and where quantity (likes, shares, followers) often overshadows the quality of connections, relationships, impact, and substance.

As a publicist and strategist, I've had the privilege of working with some of the most prominent CEOs, athletes, and thought leaders of my time. In the beginning, I followed the traditional path, focusing on visibility, crafting stories that resonated with the media, and building personal brands that caught the eye of the public. But over time, I began to realize that many of these public figures were struggling with something deeper. While they were basking in the glow of attention, something was missing and their true selves were buried beneath a mask of carefully curated content. Their digital personas didn't reflect their values, their purpose, or the impact they wanted to make. In short, they had become victims of the *optics-first* approach.

I found myself constantly grappling with a choice: *Am I helping them build something real, something meaningful? Or am I just contributing to the noise, the performative dance that leaves no lasting legacy, only fleeting moments of external validation?* I realized that I needed to find a way to shift the focus back to what truly mattered: authenticity, substance, and genuine influence. And so, I created the *'Optics-First'* Mentality, a framework to help leaders, influencers, and businesses understand the subtle dangers of prioritizing appearances over purpose, and how to make the shift toward an approach that is rooted in real impact.

This methodology is not just a critique of the digital age's obsession with optics; it's a call to action. It challenges the idea that success can only be measured by numbers and encourages us to redefine what visibility and influence should truly look like. At its core, the optics-first mentality emphasizes recognizing the difference between short-term recognition and lasting, meaningful impact. *It's about understanding that while visibility can bring opportunities, authenticity is what fosters true influence.*

A Perspective on Social Media

A Tool for Self-Expression, Not Just Validation

Now, let's talk about social media. At its best, social media exists for you, for your dreams, your expression, and your journey. It's a tool that allows you to intentionally share a part of yourself with the world. *The people who need to hear my voice or see my work should be able to find me.* It's about putting something real out there, your story, your mission, or the unique value you bring.

Social media isn't about crafting a persona to please others. Instead, it's about creating content that aligns with who you are and who you aspire to become. Your inbound content is a reflection of the person you're striving to be, the values, insights, and truths that define you. *It's about drawing in those who truly connect with my message and my values.*

Your outbound content, on the other hand, acts as the beacon. *This is my voice. This is my purpose.* It draws others in, those who are curious, those seeking what you uniquely offer, those aligned with your mission. It's not about showing off or chasing validation. Instead, it's about sharing what matters most to you, so the right people find and connect with you in meaningful ways.

In this book, I invite you to reframe your whole content mindset. Through practical exercises and thoughtful strategies, you'll learn to treat your content as a tool for authentic connection, not mere optics. Together, we'll work toward a place where your true self is visible, not where you perform for applause, but where you live for impact.

Exercise: Recognizing the 'Optics-First' Trap

Before we dive deeper into the concept and how to break free from the optics-first mentality, I want to start with a simple exercise that will help you identify whether you're currently operating from an optics-first mindset in your own life or business. By the end of this task, you'll be more attuned to the ways in which optics drive your decisions, and you'll notice how focusing solely on what your eyes alone see may be leading you astray.

Instructions

Reflect on your most recent content or actions: This could be a recent social media post, a business decision, a personal choice, or a client pitch.

Ask yourself these questions: Was the goal of this post or action to appear successful, or was it to create real value?

Did I focus on how others would perceive me, or did I focus on the impact I wanted to make?

Did I prioritize external validation such as likes, shares, comments, over internal satisfaction (personal growth, alignment with my values)?

Write down your answers: Be honest with yourself about your intentions and motivations.

Identify one example where you prioritized optics over substance: This could be a project where you sought external approval rather than focusing on long-term impact. This exercise is designed to help you tune into the subtle ways in which optics-first thinking can creep into your decision-making. By becoming aware of these tendencies, you can begin to shift your mindset and adopt a more authentic, purposeful approach to visibility and influence. The more you can spot the optics-first traps, the more control you'll have in defining your narrative both online and offline.

Chapter 1

Breaking the 'Optics-First' Mentality

"We've all been told that 'the optics' matter. But what if they didn't? What if who you are at your core, your values, your mission, was what truly mattered? Breaking free from the optics-first mentality means creating real, meaningful connections. It's about being seen for who you truly are, not just what others expect you to be or perceive from afar."
– Hannah Hall

We live in a world dominated by the optics-first mentality. Whether you're in business, sports, or even in your personal life, how things look often seems more important than what they actually are. And I understand. We've all been there. We've all been told that the right image, the right persona, the right look is what gets noticed, gets liked, and gets ahead. We're told that how we present ourselves online defines us and that, in this digital age, *perception is reality.*

But here's the truth: *that kind of thinking isn't just limiting, it's dangerous.* It forces us into boxes we don't belong in, making us conform to an image that doesn't fully reflect who we truly are. *It creates a world where we're more focused on the surface, on how things appear, rather than what they truly are.*

The rise of optics-first thinking isn't a new phenomenon, nor is it an accident. It has its roots in history, in the way publicity and marketing evolved. *Let me take you back for a moment.*

The Age of Optics – How We Got Here

Publicity, in its essence, has always been about shaping perceptions. It's about telling a story, but more importantly, it's about controlling the narrative. The origins of modern publicity trace back to the early 20th century, when figures like Edward Bernays, often called the father of public relations, began manipulating mass media to shape public opinion. Bernays understood that influencing how people thought about brands, individuals, and products wasn't just about truth, it was about perception.

In the 1920s, Bernays famously staged a campaign to encourage women to smoke. He rebranded cigarettes as *"torches of freedom"* during a time when smoking was largely considered taboo for women. This campaign led to a massive shift in how women were portrayed in media and how they viewed themselves. *It wasn't about the health risks or the social implications. It was about the image of empowerment, freedom, and modernity.*

Fast forward to today and the rise of social media has only accelerated this optics-first mentality. Platforms like Instagram, Twitter, and LinkedIn thrive on visibility—not necessarily on substance. *Likes, shares, and impressions, are the currency of today's world.* Our digital presence is so tightly intertwined with our self-worth and professional success that many of us, me included, get caught in the cycle of optics. *We're told to be everywhere, say everything, and look perfect while doing it.*

But *is that what we really want? Is that what we truly need?*

The Cost of Optics-First Thinking

Let me tell you a little secret: it's exhausting. Trying to fit into a mold of perfection, of carefully curated posts and strategic image-building, can drain your essence. *It's like a performance, one you're never truly offstage from.*

There's a price to pay when we focus too much on how things appear rather than allowing ourselves to be fully seen for who we are.

In my own work as a publicist, I've seen firsthand how *optics-first thinking* can backfire. I've worked with CEOs, athletes, and entrepreneurs who have spent years building an image that's miles away from their true selves. *The pressure to be always on, always polished, always perfect becomes unbearable.* "And when the true, authentic self is hidden behind a façade, it becomes harder to make real, meaningful connections."

But here's the beauty of it: *we can break free from this.* We can choose to value authenticity over optics. *We can choose to show up as we are, flaws and all,* and find our true connections in that honesty.

Reclaiming Authenticity

The shift from optics-first thinking to authenticity-first thinking begins with *awareness*. It starts by asking yourself *the tough questions*. It starts with making a conscious decision to show up as *your true self* not the version of you that you think others expect to see.

Exercise: Visibility Audit – What Are You Showing?

Objective: Identify the Gap between Your Online Presence and Your True Values

Take a moment to ask yourself, *what am I really showing the world?* This exercise focuses on reflection, taking stock of your digital footprint and understanding how much of it aligns with the person you are at your core. Are your posts a reflection of your mission, purpose, and story, or are they more about how they appear to others?

Here's how to explore this:
Review Your Last Five Social Media Posts or Marketing Pieces

Take a close look at your social media accounts—whether Instagram, LinkedIn, Facebook, Twitter, or any other platform you're active with and examine the last five things you've posted or shared.

Answer These Questions for Each Post:

Why did I post this? Did you post it because it was something you genuinely cared about, or was the motivation rooted in only getting attention, likes, or approval

Does it reflect my true values, mission, or story?

Consider if the content represents who you are and what you stand for, or if it aligns more with fitting into a mold.

Was this for optics (likes, impressions, approval) or authenticity (connection, education, purpose)?

Reflect on whether the post was crafted to project an image or impression, or to share something meaningful, connect with others, or educate them.

Write a Short Paragraph about Patterns or Insights You Notice

After answering these questions, step back and assess any trends. Are there posts that reflect your authentic self? Are there others that feel more performative?

Outcome: Awareness of How Well Your Content Reflects Your Values

This exercise isn't about judging you or your actions it's about awareness. Once you've completed it, you'll begin to notice where the gaps lie. You'll see how much of your content is driven by optics—the desire for approval—and how much is grounded in authenticity and purpose.

Why This Matters

I can already hear you: *"But Hannah, if I don't post the polished version, won't I get overlooked? Won't people just scroll past me?"* The truth is visibility doesn't have to mean perfection. In fact, authenticity tends to *shine* brighter than anything fabricated. The world is hungry for real stories, for genuine connection, relationships, for raw truth. If you're willing to show up as yourself, you'll attract the right people who truly connect with your message. When you break free from the optics-first mentality, you unlock the power of real visibility. And that, my friends, is what leads to lasting success, both in your personal life and in your career.

Chapter 2

The Dark Side of Visibility – Case Studies and Consequences

"Visibility is a double-edged sword. The same light that lets people see you can also cast the harshest shadows if you lose sight of who you are in the process."
– Hannah Hall

In the quest for visibility, it's tempting to believe that any attention is good attention. But not all visibility is beneficial. The relentless pursuit of optics-first visibility, whether for personal branding, business ventures, or public personas, can lead to unintended consequences. What may seem like a savvy decision in the moment can unravel, leaving reputations tarnished, credibility undermined, and individuals or brands emotionally depleted.

To truly understand the dangers of optics-driven strategies, let's explore some real-world scenarios. These case studies are not intended to incite fear; rather, they highlight the importance of authenticity and the potential pitfalls of prioritizing appearances over substance.

Case Study 1: *The Over-Curated Brand That Crumbled*

Let's talk about T*he Perfect Persona.* Picture an influencer with millions of followers. A person whose life appears flawlessly curated: immaculate homes, exotic vacations, and motivational captions under stunning, filtered selfies. They've built their empire on the promise of inspiration, success, and the illusion of having it all together.

Then one day, the façade begins to crack. It could be the result of a leaked email, a behind-the-scenes exposé, or an unedited photo revealing a reality far removed from the perfection they project. Suddenly, the figure who seemed invincible is the subject of scrutiny. Their followers feel misled.

The fallout is swift, brutal, and sometimes unforgiving. Cancel culture takes hold, amplifying the backlash. But the real devastation lies beneath the surface. In a candid interview, the influencer admits they felt imprisoned by their own brand. Vulnerability wasn't an option; imperfection wasn't allowed. The pressure to maintain a lie led to emotional and physical burnout.

Lesson Learned: A meticulously polished image may captivate at first glance, but if it isn't grounded in authenticity, it's precarious. Imperfections, when embraced, build trust and resilience. A genuine, relatable brand often outlasts one crafted to be flawless.

Case Study 2: The CEO's PR Misstep

Public relations crises often stem from a mismatch between optics and authenticity. Take the case of a CEO who, during a time of layoffs in their company, posted a LinkedIn photo of themselves on a luxury yacht with a caption about *"making hard decisions."* The post was intended to convey resilience in leadership, yet it came across as tone-deaf and out of touch.

The backlash was immediate. Employees and the public alike criticized the CEO for prioritizing personal optics over empathy for those losing their jobs. The company's reputation suffered not due to the layoffs themselves (a business reality) but because the CEO's post demonstrated a lack of alignment between their image and the values they claimed to uphold.

How could they not see this coming? many wondered. While the CEO may have believed they were exemplifying fortitude, their actions sent an entirely different message. It was a vivid reminder that perception matters just as much as intent in public relations.

Lesson Learned: Visibility without empathy can alienate the very people you're trying to connect with. It's crucial to ensure your message reflects not only your own reality but also the realities of those you serve or impact.

Case Study 3: The Athlete Who Lost Themselves

As a publicist, I've worked with athletes whose careers depend on visibility. One particular athlete I'll call "Chris" was an exceptional talent with a work ethic to match. Chris's management team was laser-focused on marketability. Their social media became a parade of sponsorships, endorsements, and *"brand-friendly"* posts.

But behind the scenes, Chris felt suffocated. *Is this really who I am now?* they often wondered. None of the posts reflected their true self. Chris loved the game but loathed the persona they'd been forced to adopt. The pressure to maintain a facade drained their enthusiasm.

Eventually, Chris decided to take a social media hiatus and started over. They began sharing authentic moments *'This is what my life actually looks like'* including the highs, the lows, and their genuine passion for the sport. The result was transformative. Their audience grew organically, connecting with Chris not just as an athlete but as a person.

The shift in approach didn't just bring Chris peace of mind; it rekindled their love for the game. They were no longer performing for approval but expressing their true self.

Lesson Learned: Athletes and professionals alike thrive when their visibility reflects their passions and personalities. Forced personas may yield short-term gains but often lead to long-term dissatisfaction and disengagement.

The Common Thread: Misalignment Between Optics and Authenticity

In each of these cases, the issue wasn't visibility itself but *how* visibility was pursued. When there's a gap between what's presented and what's real, the consequences can be disastrous. And while these examples are dramatic, the same principle applies to anyone trying to craft a digital presence. *Misalignment breeds mistrust and, worse, internal burnout.*

The antidote? *Leading with authenticity.* It's not about abandoning professionalism or strategy; it's about ensuring your visibility serves a purpose beyond approval or impressions.

Exercise: The "True Voice" Filter

Objective: Craft Content Rooted in Authenticity

This exercise focuses on finding your authentic voice while balancing professionalism. Whether you're writing a LinkedIn post, an Instagram caption, or even a press release, it's easy to fall into the trap of crafting what you think people want to hear. But what if you allowed your true self to come through? This activity will help you refine a content style that's both genuine and aligned with your values.

Instructions

Think of a topic or recent event you want to share online Choose something meaningful to you, such as a personal achievement, a reflection on current events, or a milestone in your business.

Write three versions of your post:

Version 1: Optics-First. Write the post as if you're trying to impress or appeal to your audience. Consider what might get the most likes or approval.

Example:

"Thrilled to announce I've been nominated for the Industry Leader of the Year Award! This recognition is a testament to years of hard work, resilience, and my unwavering commitment to excellence."

Version 2: No Filter. Write the post as if you're explaining it to a close friend. Forget about impressing anyone just share what's on your heart.

Example:

"I'm honestly blown away by this nomination. It feels surreal because there have been times when I doubted myself and wondered if I was making an impact. This is a reminder to keep going, even when it's hard."

Version 3: The Balance. Combine the professionalism of Version 1 with the authenticity of Version 2. Create something that reflects your values while staying true to your voice.

Example: *"I'm deeply honored to be nominated for the Industry Leader of the Year Award. It's a moment of reflection for me, a reminder of the struggles I've faced and the resilience I've built along the way. I hope this inspires others to trust the process, even when the path feels uncertain."*

Reflect on which version feels most aligned with your values.

Take a moment to read all three versions. Which one feels the most "you"? Which one conveys your message while staying true to your beliefs? Use this version as your framework moving forward.

Outcome: Communicating with Authenticity While Maintaining Professionalism

This exercise isn't about discarding professionalism. It's about creating content that feels honest and resonates with both you and your audience. With practice, it becomes easier to strike that balance, letting your true voice come through while keeping your message clear and impactful.

Visibility is powerful, but only when wielded with care.

The dark side of optics-first thinking is real, but it doesn't have to define your journey. By embracing authenticity and aligning your visibility with your values, you can avoid the pitfalls and build something that lasts.

Chapter 3

Authenticity is the New Influence – Rethinking the Rules

"In a world obsessed with looking good, the most radical act is showing up as yourself."
– Hannah Hall

In a time when likes, views, and followers are the social currency of success, authenticity has emerged as a powerful counterbalance. People are tired of the veneer, the constant push for perfection, and the emptiness of performative content. More than ever, what *resonates* is truth: a personal story that strikes a chord, a vulnerable moment shared without filters, or even a simple acknowledgment of imperfection.

Authenticity is no longer just a nice-to-have; it's becoming the most valuable currency in the digital world. Whether you're a professional, an influencer, or a brand, the ability to show up as yourself and connect on a human level is what truly creates influence that lasts.

But what does authenticity mean in practice? And how can you embrace it in a way that feels both natural and intentional? This chapter explores the shifting dynamics of influence, why authenticity matters, and how you can build meaningful connections by breaking free from the old rules.

A Brief History of Influence: From Gatekeepers to Grassroots

Before the rise of social media, influence was something reserved for the select few. Celebrities, politicians, and media personalities dominated the conversation. They controlled the narrative because they controlled the platforms. In this era, influence was top-down: you had to reach a certain level of fame or success to have a voice.

Then came the democratization of influence. Social media flipped the script, allowing anyone with a smartphone to build an audience. Suddenly, you didn't need a Hollywood studio or a glossy magazine feature to be seen or heard. All you needed was a platform and the ability to capture people's attention.

At first, this felt liberating. Small businesses thrived, marginalized voices found their platforms, and many built careers by being themselves. But as the social media landscape became crowded, the focus shifted. Algorithms rewarded the most clickable, shareable, and polished content. Over time, even the most genuine creators began to feel the pressure to curate their lives for the camera.

What we're seeing now is a reckoning. People are craving something deeper. They're tuning out the overly polished and leaning into the raw, the real, and the relatable. This is where authenticity comes in not as a trend, but as a return to what truly connects us.

The Power of Authentic Influence

At its core, influence isn't about how many people see your content; it's about how deeply it resonates with the people who see it. *Authenticity creates this resonance because it taps into shared humanity.*

Consider the content you engage with most. Is it the perfect product shot, or is it the messy behind-the-scenes post where someone shares a challenge they overcame? Is it the generic motivational quote, or is it the story of someone's personal journey, complete with all its ups and downs?

When you lead with authenticity, you invite people into your world, not just the highlight reel, but the full picture. In doing so, you give them permission to show up as themselves, too.

Rethinking the Rules of Influence

For years, the "rules" of influence have revolved around visibility and metrics. Post frequently, optimize for likes, stay on trend. But these rules don't account for substance or sustainability. They create a hamster wheel where creators feel pressured to churn out content without asking whether it's meaningful.

Here's the truth: *Influence isn't about posting more; it's about connecting more.* It's about creating content that reflects who you are, what you stand for, and how you want to serve your audience. When you approach influence this way, you're no longer chasing validation; you're building relationships.

The Three Pillars of Authentic Influence
Clarity

Authentic influence starts with knowing who you are and what you stand for. *What are your core values? What stories do you want to tell? What impact do you want to have?*

Take time to define all these attributes for yourself. Clarity gives you a foundation to build on, so you're not swayed by trends or external pressures.

- **Vulnerability**

    Being authentic doesn't mean sharing every detail of your life, but it does mean letting people perceive the real you. *Sometimes, not just your successes, also share your struggles, the lessons learnt, and the moments that shaped you.* Vulnerability isn't weakness; it's what makes your story relatable.

- **Intentionality**

    Authenticity doesn't mean posting without thought; it means being intentional and real about what you share. **Ask yourself:** W*ill this post add value to the lives of the viewers/readers? Does it align with my values? Does it reflect my true voice?*

- **The Optics-First Detox**

    To truly embrace authenticity, you have to let go of the optics-first mentality. This means shifting your focus from external validation to internal alignment. The following exercise will help you practice this shift in your own content strategy.

Exercise: The Optics-First Detox

Objective: *Experiment with breaking free from performative posting.*

For one week, your goal is to create content that focuses on substance over optics. Use this as an opportunity to reconnect with your values and rediscover the joy of sharing meaningfully.

Instructions

For one week, only post content that answers at least one of these questions:
- *Does this share a meaningful insight or personal story?*
- *Does this help or inspire others?*
- *Does this reflect my core values?*

For example, instead of posting a generic motivational quote, share a story about why that quote resonates with you. Instead of posting a polished product photo, share a behind-the-scenes look at the process behind it. At the end of the week, journal about your experience. Reflect on the following questions:
- *How did this exercise make you feel?*
- *Did you notice any changes in how people engaged with your content?*
- *Were you tempted to revert to optics-first content? Why or why not?*

Outcome

By the end of this exercise, you'll have a clearer understanding of how it feels to create content from a place of authenticity. You may also notice that your audience engages more deeply with posts that come from you heart. Most importantly, you'll have taken a step toward building influence that's meaningful and sustainable.

Authenticity in Action

The beauty of authenticity is that it doesn't just make your content better it makes you better. When you stop trying to be what you think people want and start showing up as who you are, you free yourself from the constant need for approval. You start to see visibility not as a burden, but as an opportunity to connect, relate, inspire, and make positive impact.

Chapter 4

The Publicist's Perspective – Insider Stories on the 'Game'

"Every publicist walks a fine line: the one between building someone's image and protecting your own integrity."
– Hannah Hall

When I tell people I'm a publicist, their reactions tend to fall into two categories. The first is wide-eyed intrigue, imagining me in a whirlwind of glamour, rubbing shoulders with celebrities and CEOs. The second is skepticism: *"Isn't that just spin?"*

Both reactions miss the mark. Yes, I've worked with high-profile individuals, traveled to dazzling events, and sat in boardrooms with billionaires. But publicity isn't all champagne and red carpets. At its core, my job is about storytelling—helping someone craft and communicate their narrative to the world. And like any great story, it's about balancing truth with perception.

But here's the thing: *perception can be a slippery slope.*

The Game of Elevation

Early in my career, I worked with an athlete, a rising star poised to become the face of their sport. They had the talent, the work ethic, and, most importantly, a story that could inspire. My role was to help them tell it.

At first, it was everything you'd hope for in a client relationship. They were honest about their struggles and dreams. They wanted to use their platform to make a difference. Together, we built a campaign that was as much about their personal journey as it was about their professional achievements.

And it worked. Sponsors came knocking. Media coverage soared. Their star rose, and with it, their confidence. But somewhere along the way, the spotlight started to shift their priorities.

One day, they called me about a new campaign idea. It was flashy, attention-grabbing, and completely out of alignment to how we started, with the values we had built their brand on. When I gently pushed back, reminding them of their original mission, they brushed it off.

"*Hannah,*" they said, *"it's not about that anymore. It's about staying relevant."*

That was the first time I truly felt the weight of what I do. Here was someone who had started with the best of intentions, only to lose sight of their 'why' in the glare of the spotlight. And here I was, faced with a choice: *Do I go along with it for the payday, or do I stand my ground?*

I won't pretend it was an easy decision. As a freelancer, every client matters. Bills don't pay themselves. But at the end of the day, I chose to walk away.

When the Spotlight Blinds the Mission

This wasn't the only time I've faced that choice. In fact, it's one of the most consistent challenges of being a publicist especially when you work with high-achievers like CEOs and athletes. Many come to me with noble goals: they want to inspire others, build a legacy, or use their platform for good.

But success has a way of distorting things. The more recognition they get, the more some begin to chase validation rather than meaning. They start measuring their worth in likes, headlines, and awards, forgetting the values that got them there in the first place.

One CEO I worked with perfectly embodied this tension. *They were brilliant, an innovator in their field, with a story that could have inspired an entire generation of entrepreneurs.* At the start, they were all about authenticity. They wanted to share the struggles behind their success, to show others that it wasn't all smooth sailing.

But as their profile grew, so did the pressure to maintain a certain image. They began to edit out the messier parts of their story, the failures, the moments of doubt. "It's not inspiring," they said. "People want to see success, not struggle."

I disagreed, but I went along with it for a while. The turning point came when they asked me to fabricate a story about an "aha moment" that never actually happened. It wasn't a lie, exactly, it was just a more polished version of the truth. But it felt wrong. *I told them I couldn't do it. They found someone else who could.*

Authenticity as a Strategy

Not every client takes that path. Some understand the importance of showing their real lives and building authenticity into their strategy. I've worked with athletes who share not just their victories but their injuries and setbacks. I've worked with CEOs who admit to the mistakes they've made along the way.

These are the clients who remind me why I do what I do. *They understand that influence isn't about perfection it's about connection.* And connection comes from being real.

One of my favorite stories comes from a client who was preparing for a major media interview. *They were nervous, trying to memorize talking points and rehearse answers.* I could see the stress building, so I stopped them and asked:

"What's the one thing you want people to take away from this?"

They thought about it for a moment, then said, *"I want them to know I'm just like them. I've been where they are."*

"That's your story," I said. *"Forget the script. Just tell them that."* The interview was a success, not because it was polished, but because it was heartfelt.

Lessons for Freelancers

If there's one thing I've learned in my career, it's that being a publicist or any kind of freelancer requires a strong moral compass. You'll surely be tested. You'll have clients who push you to compromise your values. There will be moments when the easy choice isn't the right one.

Here's what I'd tell anyone navigating this world:

1. Know Your Own 'Why'

Just as I ask my clients to define their values, I've had to define my own. Why do I do this work? What kind of stories do I want to tell? What kind of clients do I want to represent?

Having a clear sense of your purpose makes it easier to recognize when something doesn't align with it.

2. Set Boundaries

It's tempting to say yes to everything—especially when you're just starting out. But not every client is worth the money. If a project feels wrong, trust your gut.

3. Be the Voice of Reason

Your clients hire you for your expertise, not just your execution. Don't be afraid to push back when something doesn't feel right. Sometimes, the most valuable thing you can do is remind them of their own 'why.'

4. Don't Lose Yourself

It's easy to get caught up in the game—especially when you're helping others play it. But at the end of the day, your reputation is your greatest asset. Protect it.

The Publicist's Dilemma

Every publicist I know has faced the payday-versus-principles dilemma. It's part of the job. But I've learned that the clients who truly succeed, the ones who build influence that lasts, are the ones who stay true to themselves. And as a publicist, my job isn't just to tell your story. But also, to help you *remember* it.

Chapter 5

A Framework for Authentic Visibility–Practical Steps for Leaders

"Visibility is not about being seen; it's about being remembered for the right reasons."
– Hannah Hall

In today's world, where digital platforms dominate both professional and personal landscapes, visibility is often mistaken for success. Leaders are conditioned to believe that a polished LinkedIn post, a flashy campaign, or a viral moment equals value. But visibility built on optics alone is fragile and it lacks depth, authenticity, and sustainability.

True influence, whether in the boardroom, the locker room, or on social media, comes from a foundation of trust, integrity, and genuine connection. The challenge is learning how to break free from optics-first thinking and embrace a visibility strategy rooted in authenticity.

In this chapter we'll learn practical framework for leaders looking to elevate their personal and professional presence while staying aligned with their core values.

Breaking Free from the Optics Trap

When I started consulting for CEOs and athletes, I noticed a pattern: their primary question wasn't *"How can I make an impact?"* but rather, *"How will this look?"*

The optics-first mindset can feel safe. It's familiar and often rewarded in the short term. But it's also limiting. Leaders who focus solely on what will look good miss the opportunity to create meaningful, lasting influence.

So, how do you shift the focus? It starts with redefining what success means to you.

Step 1

Define Your Authentic Vision

Visibility without purpose is just noise. The first step toward authentic visibility is to define your vision:

What Do You Stand For?

Think beyond your professional achievements. What values guide your decisions? What causes or ideas do you care about deeply?

What Impact Do You Want to Have?

Instead of asking, *"How can I get noticed?"* ask, *"What do I want people to remember about me?"* Authentic visibility is about leaving a legacy, not just making a splash.

Who Are You Speaking To?

Visibility isn't about reaching everyone it's about resonating with the right audience to make an impact. So, identify your audience and tailor your message to connect with them on a meaningful level.

Step 2
Build a Foundation of Trust

Trust is the currency of influence. Without it, visibility is hollow. To build trust, leaders need to:

Be Transparent About Their Journey

"Share not just your successes but also your challenges, failures, and lessons learned." This humanizes you and makes your story relatable.

Engage Authentically

"It's not enough to post polished content and walk away." Respond to comments, ask questions, and foster dialogue.

Deliver Consistently

"Authenticity isn't a one-time effort; it's a commitment." Show up regularly and stay true to your message.

Step 3
Prioritize Impact Over Metrics

In the optics-first world, success is often measured by numbers: likes, views, followers, awards. But these metrics don't tell the whole story.

Instead, focus on impact:

Connections: *"Did your message resonate with someone on a deeper level?"*

Growth: *"Did the experience challenge you or help you learn something new?"*

Inspiration: *"Did you encourage others to think, feel, or act differently?"*

"A single meaningful connection is more valuable than a hundred superficial likes."

Step 4
Craft Your Narrative

Authenticity doesn't mean oversharing or losing professionalism. It's about crafting a narrative that is both genuine and intentional.

Here's how to balance the two:

Lead with Your Why

"Begin every story or message by explaining why it matters to you." This immediately adds depth and context.

Show, Don't Just Tell

Use real-life examples and anecdotes to illustrate your points. *"Facts inform, but stories inspire."*

Stay Relatable

"Whether you're addressing a team or a global audience, keep your message accessible." Avoid jargon and speak from the heart.

Step 5

Embrace Vulnerability

Vulnerability is one of the most powerful tools for building connection. Yet many leaders shy away from it, fearing it will make them appear weak.

Vulnerability makes you human, and humans are drawn to authenticity:

"Share a time when you didn't have all the answers."
"Talk about the lessons you learned from failure."
"Admit when you're still figuring things out."

This doesn't mean airing every insecurity. It's about being honest and approachable while maintaining professionalism.

Step 6

Align Actions with Words

Authenticity isn't just about what you say; it's about what you do. Leaders who consistently align their actions with their words build credibility and respect.

For example:

"If you advocate for mental health, ensure your workplace policies reflect that."

"If you champion diversity, actively seek out diverse voices in your team or network."

"Visibility without integrity will always ring hollow."

Exercise

Spot the Optics-First Pitfalls

Objective: Recognize when you're prioritizing optics over authenticity.

It's easy to fall into optics-first habits, even with the best intentions. Use this exercise to build self-awareness:

Instructions

Write Down a Professional Goal

Think of a goal you've recently worked toward (e.g., a promotion, client pitch, or social media milestone).

Reflect on These Questions:

Did I focus on what would look good or what would truly feel good? Did I measure success by numbers (likes, followers, approval) or by impact (connections, growth)?

Write One Way You Can Prioritize Meaningful Work in the Future, for example, if your goal was to gain more followers, consider focusing on creating content that sparks meaningful conversations instead.

Outcome

Greater self-awareness about optics-driven habits and a clear path to prioritizing authenticity in your future goals.

The Results of Authentic Visibility

Leaders who embrace authentic visibility often experience benefits far beyond the superficial:

Stronger Relationships: People are drawn to honesty and relatability.

Sustainable Influence: Authenticity builds a reputation that lasts.

Personal Fulfillment: When your visibility aligns with your values, you feel more confident and fulfilled.

Final Thoughts

Breaking free from optics-first thinking requires courage, introspection, and a willingness to let go of perfection. But the rewards, the deeper connections, lasting influence, and a legacy of integrity are worth it. *Authenticity isn't just a strategy; it's a commitment. And in a world that often prioritizes appearances, it's also a revolution.*

Chapter 6

Building a Legacy That Lasts— Beyond the Hashtag

"Trends are fleeting, but authenticity builds a legacy."

– Hannah Hall

In a world where digital visibility often feels like a race for attention, it's easy to mistake fleeting popularity for genuine impact. A viral post may give you a moment in the spotlight, but it's what you stand for and how you consistently live it that determines the legacy you leave behind.

The most enduring leaders, creators, and changemakers don't chase trends. Instead, they focus on aligning their online presence with their core values, building relationships that transcend platforms, and making an impact that matters long after the hashtags have faded.

This chapter explores how you can move beyond short-term optics and start crafting a legacy that truly reflects your authentic self.

The Difference Between Influence and Legacy

Influence is often defined by reach: how many people are watching, following, or liking. Legacy, on the other hand, is about depth: the meaning and value you create for others.

Here's the key distinction:

Influence is immediate. It's about the next post, the next trend, the next big moment.

Legacy is enduring. It's about the values you live by and the change you inspire over time.

While influence can feel like a sprint, building a legacy is a marathon.

Why Legacy Matters More than Trends
Trends Are Temporary

The pace of social media is relentless. Hashtags trend for a day, algorithms shift overnight, and yesterday's viral sensation is quickly forgotten. Building your brand on these fleeting moments is like constructing a house on sand.

Legacy Is Timeless

A legacy is built on principles that don't go out of style: authenticity, integrity, empathy, and purpose. *When people remember you, they won't recall your follower count or your best-performing post; they'll remember how you made them feel and the impact you had on their lives.*

Three Pillars of a Lasting Legacy

1. **Consistency**

A legacy isn't built on isolated moments but on consistent actions. Whether online or offline, stay true to your values.

"What do I want to be remembered for?" you might ask yourself. If inclusivity is a core value, ensure it's reflected in every aspect of your work from the language you use in posts to the opportunities you create for others. Consistency isn't about perfection; it's about showing up authentically every day.

Example: If inclusivity is your foundation, it should shine through in all you do. Whether it's the words you choose in your posts or the platforms you offer others, your values become the threads that weave your legacy.

2. **Impact**

Focus on the difference you make, not just the attention you gain. True impact isn't about being noticed; it's about creating change. Impact can be as simple as inspiring one person to act or as profound as transforming an entire community.

"How will my actions ripple through others?" Visualize an athlete who openly shares their struggles with mental health. By doing so, they might inspire thousands to seek help. A legacy far more meaningful than any medal.

Example: A teacher who mentors students to pursue their passions may never know the extent of their influence. But every word of encouragement, every act of guidance, becomes a seed of change.

3. **Authenticity**

A legacy rooted in pretense is easily forgotten. The more real you are, the more your story will resonate. Being authentic doesn't mean airing every vulnerability, it means aligning your actions with your true self.

"Am I sharing my truth?" CEOs, who embrace their journey, including the highs and the lows, build trust and admiration. Conversely, those who only showcase polished successes often come across as detached, leaving their audience uninspired.

Example: A writer who shares the struggles of rejection and perseverance may connect deeply with aspiring authors. Their transparency becomes a beacon of hope, showing others that success is attainable, even through setbacks.

Exercise

The Mirror Test

Objective: *Align your online presence with your true self.*

It's easy to present a version of yourself online that fits into the mold of what's popular or expected. But does that version reflect the person you are offline?

Instructions

Imagine a close friend or mentor reviewing your last 10 posts.

Think about someone who knows you deeply, your values, quirks, struggles, and strengths.

Ask these questions:

Would they see the real me in these posts?

Is there a disconnect between who I am offline and how I present myself online?

Write one way you can close that gap in future posts.

For example:

If your posts feel overly polished, share a behind-the-scenes moment that shows your personality.

If your content focuses on achievements, balance it with lessons learned from failures or challenges.

Outcome

By reflecting on your current presence and taking intentional steps to close the gap, you'll align your personal brand with your authentic self.

Lessons from the Field: Authentic Legacy Builders

In my years of working with CEOs, athletes, and change makers, I've seen firsthand what sets lasting legacies apart from fleeting fame. Here are a few standout **Examples:**

The CEO Who Led with Vulnerability

One client, a tech CEO, was initially hesitant to share personal stories. But when they opened up about the challenges of balancing work and family, their posts resonated more deeply than any corporate milestone ever had. It wasn't the accolades they'd won that inspired people; it was their humanity.

The Athlete Who Inspired Beyond the Field

A Paralympic gold medalist I worked with didn't just share their victories. They talked about the struggles, the training setbacks, and the moments of doubt. Their authenticity created a community of followers who saw them as more than an athlete, they became a symbol of resilience.

The Leader Who Put Impact First

Another client, a founder of a sustainable fashion brand, used their platform to educate their audience about the environmental cost of fast fashion. Instead of chasing likes, they focused on sparking meaningful conversations, and as a result, built a loyal and engaged community.

These individuals understood that their legacy wasn't about looking good in the moment; it was about staying true to their values over time.

Practical Steps for Building Your Legacy
Identify Your North Star

Your legacy should be guided by a clear purpose. *What is the one thing you wish to be remembered for?*

Focus on Quality Over Quantity

It's better to create one meaningful post that inspires action than ten that are forgettable.

Think Beyond Yourself

A legacy isn't just about personal success; it's about the difference you make in the lives of others.

Celebrate the Journey

Document not just where you are now but how you got there. Share the moments of growth, the lessons learned, and the people who helped along the way.

Let Go of Perfection

Perfection is an illusion. *People don't connect with flawless; they connect with reality.*

The Reward of Authenticity

When you focus on creating a legacy rather than chasing trends, something remarkable happens:

Your audience becomes more engaged because they trust you.

Your work feels more fulfilling because it aligns with your values.

Your influence extends beyond platforms, creating a ripple effect of positive change.

Final Thoughts

Building a legacy that lasts requires patience, intention, and courage. It's about showing up authentically, even when it's tempting to conform to the latest trend. It's about prioritizing substance over optics and impact over appearances.

As you reflect on your own journey, ask yourself:
What do I want to stand for?
How can I align my actions with my values?

What legacy do I want to leave behind?

The answers to these questions will serve as your compass, guiding you toward a visibility strategy that authentically represents who you are. By staying true to your values and aspirations, you can create a lasting impact on the world around you.

Chapter 7

Leading by Example

Before the Shift: The Performative Visibility Trap

Before embracing purpose-driven engagement, many of these leaders found themselves ensnared in a relentless cycle of *performative visibility*. The pressure to appear successful, likable, or knowledgeable without genuinely adding value.

Here's how this often manifested:

Superficial Metrics: They fixated on follower counts, likes, and comments, equating *popularity with influence.*

Curated Perfection: Their content became polished to the point of *inauthenticity,* showcasing only highlights and leaving no space for vulnerability or the messiness of real-life struggles.

Visibility for Validation: Their actions were driven by a yearning for *external approval* rather than a deeply rooted intention to create meaningful impact.

Disconnected from Values: Much of their content strayed from their *true mission and core values,* instead catering to what was trendy or perceived as relevant.

Why did so many leaders fall into this trap? The digital world's obsession with optics and appearances played a significant role. Yet, as time passed, they began to see the cracks in this approach. It was unsustainable, unfulfilling, and devoid of the transformative change they sought. Moreover, it failed to cultivate genuine, lasting relationships with their audience.

After the Shift: Purpose-Driven Engagement

In contrast, these leaders have embraced a radically different approach one that centers on authenticity, impact, and meaningful connection.

Here's what their strategies now embody:

Value-Driven Content: They share content aligned with their *mission and core values,* prioritizing education, inspiration, and storytelling that genuinely serve their audience.

Vulnerability and Authenticity: Perfection is no longer the goal. They present the *full spectrum of their journey,* including struggles, setbacks, and personal growth moments that others can relate to.

Impact Over Appearances: Success is no longer measured by *approval or applause* but by the tangible difference they create. The depth of their relationships and the quality of their contributions are what matter most.

Building Trust: By being consistent, transparent, and purpose-driven, they've built a foundation of *trust*. Their authenticity carries more weight than the most polished post ever could.

8. More Practical Exercises (for the Back of the Book)

Here are some exercises you can include at the end of your book to help readers put the principles from this chapter into action. These exercises will guide them in building a content strategy and brand identity that prioritizes *authenticity* over *optics*.

The "Substance-First" Content Grid

Objective: Develop a content plan that prioritizes impact over appearances.

Instructions:

Prepare a sheet of paper or create a spreadsheet divided into four quadrants:

Educate: Share knowledge or insights that teach your audience something new.

Inspire: Tell a story or share a meaningful lesson that encourages action and motivation.

Connect: Be open, relatable, and authentic by expressing vulnerability or shared experiences.

Showcase: Highlight your achievements or work, but go beyond appearances by explaining their deeper significance.

Brainstorm one idea for each quadrant. Create content around these ideas and post over the next month.

Outcome:

A thoughtfully balanced content strategy that emphasizes authenticity, builds meaningful connections, and creates lasting impact.

Your Authentic Brand Story

Objective: Articulate your values and mission in a way that feels authentic and true to you.

Instructions:

Reflect and answer these questions:

What three values guide everything I do?

What personal or professional story defines why I do this work?

What do I want people to remember about me or my brand?

Use your answers to craft a concise and impactful one-paragraph mission statement or tagline.

Outcome:

A clear, authentic statement that reflects your values and mission, suitable for use in your marketing and communications to establish a strong, relatable brand presence.

Reframe Your Wins

Objective: Celebrate accomplishments with authenticity.

Instructions:

Reflect on a recent achievement you've shared (or wanted to share).

Draft two versions of how you'd communicate this success:

Version 1: Focus solely on optics by emphasizing awards, numbers, or buzzwords.

Version 2: Dive into the story behind the win, highlighting what it taught you, who it helped, and why it mattered.

Compare both versions to determine which resonates more with your values and approach.

Outcome:

Gain a deeper understanding of how to frame your accomplishments in ways that prioritize authenticity, add meaningful depth, and connect with your audience on a personal level.

Meaningful Metrics Tracker
Objective: Measure Success Beyond Numbers
Instructions:

Define 3-5 meaningful metrics for your personal brand or business. Examples include:

New relationships built.

Quality of conversations.

Projects that align with your values.

Track these metrics consistently for a month.

Reflect on how focusing on substance, rather than purely numerical outcomes, impacts your goals and decision-making.

Outcome:

A thoughtful shift in perspective of what success truly mean to you.

By incorporating these exercises into your daily routine, you will craft a brand rooted in authenticity, substance, and meaningful impact—just like the leaders highlighted in this chapter. Your journey to leading by example is only beginning, and these tools will guide you in building a legacy that lasts.

Conclusion

The Final Shift – From Influence to Impact

As you close the last page of this book, take a moment to reflect on everything you've learned about authenticity, leadership, and the true power of influence. *We've explored the pitfalls of performative visibility, the art of crafting purpose-driven content, and the real stories of leaders who have transformed their public personas.* But here's the ultimate truth: *the most powerful shift you can make in your career and life isn't just about the content you post or the image you project, it's about the ripple effect you create when you shift your focus from being seen to creating meaning.*

True leaders don't need a stage to shine. *Their impact is measured in the quiet moments, the lives they touch, and the small gestures that ripple outward.* It's in the honesty they bring to their work, the courage to show vulnerability, and the relentless pursuit of their purpose, no matter how much noise surrounds them.

This book is not just a guide on how to show up authentically in your career or personal brand; *it's a blueprint for how to live a life of lasting impact.* Long after your social media posts have faded from the screen, *the influence you've created can continue to shape the world.*

Here's the unusual and powerful challenge I leave you with: *What if, for the rest of your life, you chose to lead not by how visible you are, but by how deeply you can make someone else feel seen?*

What if your ultimate measure of success wasn't how many followers you amassed or how many likes your posts received, but how many people felt inspired, uplifted, or empowered by your journey, your story, and your willingness to show the world who you truly are?

The future of influence lies not in striving for perfection or external validation but in embracing the courage to be imperfect, real, and deeply connected. *When you align your actions, content, and goals with your true self, you become a beacon for others, not just a figure they admire, but someone who changes the way they see themselves and their own potential.*

So, let your authenticity shine through every word you speak, every post you share, and every step you take. And remember *true influence isn't about being at the top of the mountain. It's about helping others climb alongside you.* You've now been equipped with the tools and insights to build your own legacy of impact. *It's time to get to work, to live out your purpose, and to lead by example.* Let's make the shift from optics to authenticity and change the game forever.

www.ingramcontent.com/pod-product-compliance
Lightning Source LLC
Chambersburg PA
CBHW070412230526
45471CB00006B/2762